COVIDIOTS

COVIDIOTS

Stories of idiotic acts
and bizarre behaviour

Steven Richard Harris
Natalia Gómez Álvarez

This book is dedicated to all those that have suffered or continue to suffer from COVID-19 and its terrible consequences.

With love to Gary, Eunhye and Leo.

CONTENTS

INTRODUCTION...1

1   Opposites attract...3

2   Robin Hood...7

3   Garlic breath..10

4   Permission to land.....................................12

5   Raining cats and dogs.................................15

6   One for the road.......................................18

7   Roll with it 21

8   Keep calm and....drink   vodka 26

9   Herd immunity 29

10   Be-retching curfew....................................32

11   Easy riders 34

12   Off the rails...37

13   Airport run...40

14   From my cold dead hands 43

15   Up in smoke..46

16   Mayor Dummkopf 48

17   Something fishy...51

18   Instant karma 55

19   Technophobia..58

20   You gotta fight for   your right to party 61

21   Walking with dinosaurs 64

22   Bite the hand that feeds.............................66

23 YES, PRIME MINISTER 69

24 Man´s best friend 72

25 Shame on you 76

26 We shall not be moved 80

27 Follow the leader 83

28 Rudy idiot 88

29 Minister of (no) defense 91

30 Dirty cash 95

31 Free hugs 98

32 Love in a time of Coronavirus 102

33 They shall not pass 105

34 The show must go on 110

35 Trump 112

36 Don´t try this at home 119

Appendix 124

INTRODUCTION

Firstly, we want to make it very clear that this book was not written with even the slightest intention to cause offense to anyone in any way.

The Coronavirus pandemic was, and continues to be, a humanitarian crisis that has cost the lives of many thousands of people, both directly and indirectly. Our deepest sympathy goes out to those who passed away, lost loved ones, or had their hopes and dreams destroyed by this terrible tragedy.

In the first few months of 2020, we read or watched heart-breaking stories of the fight for life against this invisible enemy, many of which moved us deeply. When we tried to understand the magnitude of the situation we realized that we had to look for a little hope and humour at this dark moment and, if we could, share the stories that we found.

And so, confined to our apartment in northern Spain in April 2020, after managing to make it back by the skin of our teeth while on honeymoon in New Zealand just hours before they locked up the country and threw away the key, we found ourselves recovering from our four-day, three-continent-spanning journey writing this simple book.

Escaping from so many sad news stories full of figures of the infected and, unfortunately, death tolls that numbered in the many thousands, we spent our time looking for those hidden gems that would bring us that little bit of humour that is needed to look on the bright side of life. Some stories we found, although not being exactly what you could call funny, are so hard to believe that we thought they should be included here.

Please excuse us if there seems to be bias towards news articles from Spain, Britain and New Zealand, as our close links to these countries made us follow events from these places avidly. Our apologies, (or maybe not) if we haven´t included examples of covidiots from your country.

Steven Richard Harris & Natalia Gómez Álvarez
Oviedo, 05th April. 2020

1 OPPOSITES ATTRACT

Isolation can inspire people, it´s true. Many great ideas are a result of people being stuck indoors for one reason or another. Mary´s Shelly´s Frankenstein, for example, is believed to have been written as the author was sheltering indoors due to the consequences of a faraway volcanic eruption. It is also no coincidence that weather-beaten Scotland and Finland can lay claim to a huge number of inventions throughout history.

However, Australian astrophysicist Dr Daniel Reardon does not really fit into the above category.

After learning that COVID-19 could be transmitted by touching your face with infected hands, Dr Reardon set about using his knowledge of pulsars and gravitational waves in order to invent a device that would help prevent the spread of the coronavirus. Using powerful neodymium magnets attached to wristbands and a necklace, the gadget was designed to buzz every time your hand went near your face, thus preventing you from transmitting the virus from your hands to your eyes or mouth. Not a bad idea in theory, but unfortunately it didn´t work exactly as this budding inventor wanted and he scrapped the idea.

So, what does any PhD-qualified astrophysicist/inventor do next? In his own eloquent words:

"*I was still a bit bored, playing with the magnets. It's the same logic as clipping pegs to your ears – I clipped them to my earlobes and then clipped them to my nostril and things went downhill pretty quickly when I clipped the magnets to my other nostril.*"

Things went downhill indeed. Dr Reardon then placed two magnets inside his nostrils, and two on the outside. When he removed the magnets from the outside of his nose, the two inside got stuck to each other and wouldn't budge.

"*After struggling for 20 minutes, I decided to Google the problem and found ...the solution was more magnets. To put on the outside to offset the pull from the ones inside.*"

He continues to explain his actions.

"*As I was pulling downwards to try and remove the magnets, they clipped on to each other and I lost my grip. In addition, those two magnets ended up in my left nostril while the*

5

other one was in my right. At this point I ran out of magnets."

With no more magnets left, he naturally turned to a pair of pliers to try to free the ones stuck up his nose.

"Every time I brought the pliers close to my nose, my entire nose would shift towards the pliers and then the pliers would stick to the magnet," he said. *"It was a little bit painful at this point."*

He had no other choice but to go to the nearest hospital, (where, incidentally, his partner works) to get the magnets taken out. After having a good laugh at their colleague´s partner, doctors finally removed the magnets, and in a possible medical first, stated that the incident was due to *"isolation and boredom"*.

The official medical report concluded with the words: *"denies difficulty breathing, denies further magnets."*

2 ROBIN HOOD

The COVID-19 crisis has made many people consider some professions as "heroes", with health-service workers, cleaning staff and emergency services being at the top of the list.

Could one do-gooder in Manchester, England be included on this list with his real-life Robin Hood deeds? Or is he just another covidiot?

The self-proclaimed hero, going by the name "Outlaw", previously came to the public´s attention by handing out cash to homeless people in Manchester. Now in times of greater need, he has taken to the streets of the north-western British city again to hand out what he refers to as *"lockdown essentials".*

Crawling along the roads with Bobby McFerrins´s "Don´t Worry Be Happy" blaring out of a van with a homemade sign reading *"Free Isolation Essentials. Toilet Roll - Sanitizer - Bottled Water. Mini Grinders - Raws - Pre Rolls - Bud"*, the balaclava-wearing Outlaw claims *"spreading positivity at this dark and uncertain time is necessary."*

On the 03rd April 2020, he said, "*This week I've given away over 300 packs of toilet roll, four ounces of cannabis, hundreds of small sanitiser pots and six large crates of bottled water.*"

At a time when hand sanitisers are being sold on the black market for astronomical prices, and people are fighting over packets of two-ply at the supermarkets, maybe it´s time for a bit of covidiocy from the likes of Outlaw, the Robin Hood of Manchester.

3 GARLIC BREATH

We all know the health benefits that garlic brings, which is something that has led it to be used in traditional medicine and as a health supplement for centuries around the world.

In these COVID-19 times, people are looking for all kinds of ways to boost their immune system and adding a little extra garlic or taking a pill or two may help you stay healthy.

However, one woman in the Chinese province of Zhjiang took things to the next level. Having read that raw garlic can help in the fight against the coronavirus, Ms Zhang went about eating over 1.5 kg of the stuff over the course of two weeks. Far from making her feel healthier, her throat swelled up to the point that she couldn´t speak, her breathing became difficult and she believed she was suffering a fever.

After being admitted to hospital for checks, and testing negative for the coronavirus, doctors concluded that she had no severe health issues but, using a term quite common in traditional Chinese medicine, *"a lot of inner heat"* from eating so much of the bulbous vegetable.

She was discharged from hospital and spent the next few days recovering at home with her husband – presumably in separate rooms.

4   PERMISSION TO LAND

As COVID-19 spread around the world, governments took measures, mostly in vain, to try to prevent the virus reaching their shores. Some nationalities were prohibited, most flights were cancelled, and many foreigners were asked (sometimes not so politely) to return to their country of origin.

Various governments around the world tried to organise flights in order to bring home those citizens who found themselves in places where normal commercial airlines had stopped operating or where it would cost a kidney or two to buy a plane ticket to get them back.

One such place was Ecuador, which had banned travel to and from the country but still allowed repatriation flights to pick up tourists who had found themselves stuck far from home, funds fast disappearing and with little option but to raid the dwindling supplies of their hotel mini bars to survive.

On the morning of 19th March 2020, two flights originating from Madrid and Amsterdam, occupied solely by their flight crews, were making their way to pick up their stranded compatriots. After around ten hours of flying, as they were making their final approach to the airport in Ecuador's most populous city, Guayaquil, they were shocked to be advised that a flotilla of council trucks and vans were parked strategically along the length of the runway in a scene that wouldn't look out of place in a *Die Hard* movie.

Guayaquil's mayor, and official covidiot, Cynthia Viteri, had ordered, in defiance of the central government, that the airport be stormed and the runway blocked by her army of council workers "*in defense of the city*".

The flights were subsequently redirected to Quito and despite her best efforts in international relations and her desperate attempts to keep the potentially disease-spreading flight crews out, Ms Viteri´s city still found itself sadly overwhelmed with COVID-19 cases as the virus took hold throughout March and April.

5 RAINING CATS AND DOGS

Wherever the real origin of COVID-19 lies, it is clear that the virus first came to the world´s attention when Chinese authorities alerted the World Health Organisation on 31st December 2019 to several cases of "*an unusual pneumonia*" in Wuhan, a port city of 11 million people in the central Hubei province.

The source of the virus was believed to be a "wet market" in Wuhan, as many of the workers there were suffering from symptoms we now recognise as typical of COVID-19. Rumours abound about the origin, although many researchers believe that bats are the true culprits.

As we all know, in Chinese culture it is common to eat a wide variety of animals and insects that many people in the "western" world may find a bit difficult to stomach. Obviously, to most people, the Chinese were not infecting themselves by biting heads off bats à la Ozzy Osbourne, but rather it is thought that chickens or other live animals sold at the market in Wuhan were infected by the flying mammals and in turn passed the virus on to humans.

This link to animal-human zoonotic contagion led to many experts making their opinions known to the public on the matter. In one such interview with *China Central*

Television, Dr Li Lanjuan, a leading epidemiologist and hepatologist at Zhejiang University School of Medicine, stated that, "*If pets come into contact with suspected patients, they should be quarantined.*"

However, local media outlet *Zhibo China* reportedly changed her words into the rather blunt, "*cats and dogs can spread the coronavirus*".

After the rumour was posted on the social media platform Weibo, the news spread like wildfire. In the wake of the doctor´s twisted comments, reports came in the following day of dogs and cats thrown from tower blocks, with one dog found dead in Tianjin City in China's Hebei Province and five cats reported to have been thrown from flats in Shanghai.

Whoever the real covidiots are in this story, it is clear that they were the first in a long line of future morons that would react to the COVID-19 crisis in some quite idiotic and often cruel ways.

6 ONE FOR THE ROAD

One of the most shared stories on the internet during the initial outbreak of COVID-19 was the news that many Americans were turning their backs on the Mexican beer brand Corona.

While many people believe that this was fake news designed to belittle the intelligence of those from the United States, a survey was in fact undertaken (albeit with just 737 participants) in which it was found that 38% of people questioned would not buy Corona beer "*under any circumstances*".

Other findings from the survey stated that among regular Corona drinkers, only 4% said they would stop drinking the brand, 14% said they wouldn't order Corona in a public venue, and 16% of beer-drinking Americans were confused about whether Corona beer was related to the coronavirus.

What is unclear, though, are the reasons for the 38% for not drinking the tasty beverage, as the survey did not provide this interesting information. That leads us to speculate many hypotheses, from fear of being infected by the CORONAvirus, to fear of products deriving from the other side of Trump´s wall, to fear of …well, practically everything relatively unknown.

Whatever the personal reasons this small cross-section of American beer-drinking society had for not buying Corona beer, sales nationwide actually rose by 5% in February 2020.

However, production eventually ground to a halt at the start of April as the Mexican government deemed it a non-essential product.

Pity.

7 ROLL WITH IT

E ver since Robert Capa captured photos of the Spanish Civil War at the end of the 1930s, images released by the mass media have gone hand in hand with historic world events. Nick Ut´s "Napalm girl" of the Vietnam War, the lone protestor in front of a tank in Tiananmen Square, and the "Dust lady" in the aftermath of the 9/11 attacks all spring to mind.

What though, will be the everlasting image of the COVID-19 crisis? Maybe it will be the lines of patients waiting to be treated in the corridors of one of the many hospitals around the world, or the harrowing images of the intensive care unit in Lombardy, Italy? One of the many banners of hope perhaps, draped over a balcony while people are confined to their houses, or possibly even the microscopic image of the spiky-haired virus itself?

None of the above I´m afraid. It will undoubtedly be a photo of empty shelves in a supermarket that has sold out of toilet paper.

Some of the most talked-about and shared stories from the COVID-19 crisis were those of people stockpiling loo roll or fighting for the last packets in the stores while others around them filled trolleys to the brim with as many rolls as they could possibly fit into their SUVs.

Other stories that went viral were the sale and purchase of the product on the black market at prices that are normally reserved for gold and saffron, or the blocking up of city drains as people bunged up pipes with wet wipes.

There is of course, nothing more harrowing during the end of humanity than to imagine being down to your last few sheets while the world descends into chaos around you.

How the 70-75% percent of the world´s population that never uses toilet paper copes without this life-saving commodity is beyond comprehension.

In fact, studies have been carried out as to why the remaining 25-30% of us in the "developed" world found it so necessary to fill our spare room with so much toilet paper. One consumer psychologist suggests that "*people need to do something practical to feel like they are in control of the situation*", and that "*seeing photos of empty shelves online fuels a further vicious circle*".

Whatever the reasons are, it is clear that toilet paper has become such a sought-after commodity that it has led to some extreme behaviour, such as the armed robbery of a delivery van in Hong Kong, and the constant theft of toilet paper from the trolley of a blind Australian woman while shopping in Melbourne.

Another case was of one guy, also in Australia funnily enough, who now has 5,400 rolls he intended to sell online for a small fortune. Thanks to covidiots like him, many customers were rationed to just one packet per person at Aussie supermarkets. He has been subsequently black-listed from all online trading sites and is now sharing his flat with a piles of the product he can´t get rid of.

We´ve also seen examples of people trying to take matters into their own hands and shaming those buying more than they need, like the woman in the USA who angrily confronted a youth in a supermarket with two carts full of toilet paper, seemingly taking even more from the shelves in front of him. Pulling him around to face her, ready to give him a piece of her mind, her eyes were drawn down to the name badge pinned to his uniform and the handheld barcode scanner swinging from his wrist.

8   KEEP CALM AND....DRINK VODKA

If there were a prize for the biggest Covidiot out there then Alexander Lukashenko, the burly leader of Belarus, would stand a pretty good chance of winning it.

Thanks to Lukashenko´s outspoken manner and bravado in the face of the pandemic, he´s given us enough material to work with here that we don't really need to write much ourselves for this page. So sit back with a nice glass of Smirnoff and enjoy some of his best moments:

"It's better to die standing than live on your knees."

"There are no viruses here."

"Sport, especially the ice, this 'fridge' – it's the best anti-virus medicine." (Referring to an ice rink after an ice-hockey match)

"Wash your hands more often, have breakfast, lunch and dinner on time and, though I'm not a drinker, I joke now that you shouldn't just wash your hands with vodka, but each day have the equivalent of 40-50 millilitres of pure alcohol to poison this virus."

27

"But don´t drink at work."

"Go to the sauna, that's also healthy once or twice a week."

"There's no need for any panic. We just need to work, especially in the countryside. On television it's nice to see people working there on the tractor, no one's talking about viruses."

"The tractor will cure everyone there, the fields cure everyone."

Thank you Mr Lukashenko.

9 HERD IMMUNITY

With most towns and cities in the world bereft of people, many animals took advantage of the absence of humans and traffic to explore areas normally off-limits to them.

In Wales, a country more famous for sheep (and Tom Jones), a herd of long-haired Kashmiri goats took over the deserted town centre in Llandudno, in the north of the country, a town normally only visited by British tourists attracted by the Victorian Pier, Bodafon Farm Park petting zoo, and Bonkerz Fun Centre.

With the arrival of the striking Kashmiri goats, which normally graze on the beautiful Great Orme promontory outside of the town, Llandudno was thrust into the international media spotlight.

The goats invaded front gardens, strolled down the high street admiring their own reflections in shop windows, did a few laps of the cemetery at the local church, and even dozed in the vicar´s private parking space. All while amused locals peered out of their windows and filmed them on their mobile phones.

They became an online hit with many people sheltering at home around the world, desperate for some light-hearted news to brighten up their confinement or looking for alternatives to entertaining their children, decorating the spare bedroom, or (if lucky enough to find yeast and flour in the supermarkets) baking yet more biscuits and cakes.

As the goats nibbled on perfectly-trimmed privet hedges and prize-winning roses, they were blissfully unaware of the joy they brought to hundreds of thousands of people watching and sharing their uploaded images and of the chaos that was unfolding around the world outside of sleepy Llandudno.

10   BE-RETCHING CURFEW

As a third of the world´s population entered some form of lockdown during March 2020, the number of people defying their government´s orders to stay at home steadily started to grow.

Most people stopped by the police in countries like Spain, either had to have permission to be outside in order to undertake some kind of essential task, or had to accept the caution or fine that was given to them for breaking the curfew if they had no such excuse.

However, some people were not so understanding with the police.

In the southern Spanish city of Malaga, one woman was arrested after police were called to the scene of an argument between a port security guard and the woman in question. Not content with just throwing objects at the security guard and the police officers, she then attempted another form of hurling.

While being detained, the woman starting kicking, spitting and finally with no other recourses left, tried her best to vomit on the officers.

It is not clear if she was successful in her attempts nor the methods used in order to provoke the regurgitation, but what is known is that she was charged with public order offenses and assaulting the police officers involved in the fracas.

11   EASY RIDERS

Where in the world is it possible to escape the COVID-19 madness?

If you thought that New Zealand, (an isolated island nation far away from the virus epicentres of the USA, Europe and China, with vast open spaces and a small population spread out among beautiful countryside) might be the place, think again.

Despite not having suffered an initial outbreak of COVID-19 as serious as some other places in the rest of the world, due in part to strict measures having been taking relatively early, much of the population followed the trend of panic-buying seen elsewhere, resulting in empty shelves and long queues snaking around the outside of supermarkets.

We´ve already witnessed some quite heated arguments between shoppers in various places, but our search for covidiots brought us to the cheap and cheerful supermarket chain, Pak n´ Save in the eastern city of Napier.

A sleepy town of just 65,000 inhabitants, the beautifully restored art deco capital of New Zealand is not the place you would expect to find a biker gang feud.

However, it appears that gang warfare may be on the horizon, due to events at the Napier supermarket, all because of .... a frozen chicken.

As members of the notorious biker gangs The Mongrel Mob and Black Power both reached for the last bag of frozen chicken, it was clear that there would be trouble.

Thankfully, police officers were called to the scene to break up the fight that was starting to get out of hand in the frozen food aisle, and no one was seriously injured in the incident.

Locals are now hoping this is not the spark that ignites a more serious battle between the gangs, who have had some rather violent quarrels over the years to say the least.

It is not clear who ended up with the last bag of chicken.

12 OFF THE RAILS

When governments declare state of emergencies, businesses are forced to close and the general public are prohibited from going about their normal daily lives. Something which means that conspiracy theories abound.

So, what do you do if you believe that there is more to a situation than meets the eye? Share your thoughts with your friends? Call a radio phone-in? Write a blog? Or try to crash a train into a hospital ship?

Unbelievably, the last option is exactly what Eduardo Moreno did on the 01st April 2020 at the Port of Los Angeles.

Sounding more like an April Fool´s joke, train operator and engineer, Moreno was filmed holding a lit flare in the cab of the 200-tonne locomotive as he sent it crashing into a steel barrier, through a chain-link fence, across a parking lot, and then into another fence before stopping just 250 metres from the U.S.N.S Mercy hospital ship, deployed in the port to alleviate congestion in hospitals due to COVID-19.

Covidiot Moreno, suspicious of the ship´s real intentions and why the government had sent it to the area, did not believe that *'the ship is what they say it's for"* and is quoted as saying, *"You only get this chance once. The whole world is watching. I had to. People don't know what's going on here. Now they will."*

Mr Moreno will probably now have quite a bit of time to think up more conspiracy theories as he was charged with one count of train-wrecking. An offense carrying up to 20 years in prison.

13 AIRPORT RUN

On the 14th March 2020, The Spanish government declared a state of emergency and prohibited the opening of any non-essential businesses and travel. One of the hardest-hit countries by COVID-19, Spain introduced these measures in order to try to prevent the spread of the deadly virus, which was spiralling out of control.

With eerily empty streets, police roadblocks and airports receiving 90% less passengers at this time, many Spanish areas were effectively ghost towns.

Nevertheless, two covidiots obviously didn't get the memo.

On 20th March at around 5am, the duo smashed their Renault Captur through revolving doors into the foyer of terminal 1 at Barcelona's usually bustling El Prat airport, presumably intent on causing as much carnage as possible.

The handful of cleaning staff present at the time, tasked with disinfecting duties, were reported to have heard one of the men shout *"Allahu Akbar",* and as the sound of this proclamation to God echoed around the virtually deserted terminal building, the men were swiftly arrested by the security services stationed there.

The two men, of Albanian descent, were found to be under the influence of *"mind altering substances"* at the time, to such an extent that one had to be hospitalized, using up vital medical resources and a bed at the most desperate of times.

Let´s hope they are forced to spend their own type of self- isolation for a considerable amount of time to come.

14 FROM MY COLD DEAD HANDS

In March 2020, we witnessed the start of panic buying around the world as people stockpiled lockdown essentials like toilet paper and hand sanitiser. Shoppers queued for hours outside supermarkets to make sure they had enough supplies to get them through these tough times.

We saw lines of people trying to get into pharmacies around the world too as cold and flu remedies and Vitamin C flew off the shelves.

But what do people really need in times of lockdown? What will keep that pesky COVID bug away from you?

The answer is of course a gun. Not just one gun, but 3.7 million. That´s the number of firearms background checks that were carried out in the month of March in the United States, and with individuals able to buy multiple weapons, the figure of actual gun sales was probably much higher.

Maybe we´re mocking this form of panic buying unjustly. Maybe the virus will mutate and those armed with a semi-automatic will be the lucky ones to survive the zombie apocalypse. Maybe they will be the chosen few, closely guarding their last precious sheets of toilet paper as hordes of the unclean desperately search for a last piece of dignity in a world lacking basic hygiene.

It´s not just in the States that gun sales skyrocketed though. Even in the apparently mild-mannered nation of New Zealand, queues of people were seen outside gun stores as the country prepared for lockdown.

Anti-Chinese sentiment was growing in some quarters in "the land of the long white cloud", leading to the sale of firearms increasing among Asian residents as they threatened to form militia groups to protect themselves against a possible backlash for being "responsible" for bringing the virus to New Zealand's shores.

Utter madness.

15 UP IN SMOKE

Back in China, where COVID-19 is believed to have broken out, many citizens took to some inventive measures in order to try to protect themselves from picking up the virus.

You probably saw images on the television or internet of people wearing 5-litre water bottles stuck on their heads or grapefruit halves being used as face masks.

Of course, during the height of the COVID-19 outbreak, PPE (Personal Protective

Equipment) was like gold dust, not just in China, but also throughout the rest of the world, even among the professional health services of many countries.

Citizens were therefore left to their own devices to protect themselves and sterilize their surroundings with whatever came to hand.

One unfortunate woman in Hefei, in the south-eastern province of Anhui, trying to avoid being infected with COVID-19, sprayed as much rubbing alcohol (surgical spirit) as she could over herself thinking that it would protect her from the lethal virus.

Heading back into the kitchen to tend to the food that she had left on the stove, the alcohol, which still hadn´t absorbed into the material of her clothes, ignited due to the close proximity of the open flame, causing an explosion that left the poor woman hospitalized and with severe burns to her hands and face.

16   MAYOR DUMMKOPF

We all know that politicians say some quite idiotic things sometimes, especially when elections are looming. We also know that very often actions speak louder than words and it´s what you do rather than what you say that matters.

With that in mind, let´s judge the actions of one local politician from Germany. More specifically, Green Party politician Stephan von Dassel, 53, Mayor of Berlin´s Mitte district.

Acting as a perfect role model in a crisis, he did what any great leader would do to inspire his followers and instil courage in a time of need. He deliberately got himself infected with COVID-19.

OK, there must be a good reason, I hear you say. In Herr Dassel´s own words:

"I did get myself intentionally infected, IN ORDER TO AMUSE MYSELF."

Hilarious indeed. He continues:

"And I thought, well you know, for three days be a bit out of sorts, and then with immunity I can't be infected again, and also can't infect anyone else - But it was worse than I thought."

In his defense, this covidiot´s claim that he had a duty to make sure he was healthy in the long term by becoming immune to the virus, was something other politicians have dabbled unsuccessfully with during the course of the COVID-19 pandemic.

Needless to say, this local politician has not won any popularity contests among constituents and health professionals in his native Germany and will surely be known as the EX-mayor of Mitte district, Berlin, in the not too distant future.

17   SOMETHING FISHY

In a White House briefing on March 20th 2020, President Trump extolled the virtues of two drugs used to treat malaria; chloroquine and hydroxychloroquine, stating that chloroquine in particular could be a *"game changer"* in the fight against the coronavirus.

The drug in question, chloroquine, cannot only be found in malaria treatments but also in medicines used to treat lupus, and surprisingly, in some fish-tank cleaning products.

Former *Apprentice* host, Trump, added that chloroquine had shown *"very, very encouraging early results"* and incorrectly that the U.S Food and Drug Administration had approved the drug by saying, *"it's been approved … So we're going to be able to make that drug available by prescription."*

Later, Trump´s itchy little thumbs couldn´t help themselves as he added on Twitter that taken with a combination of a certain antibiotic, chloroquine could be *"one of the biggest game changers in the history of medicine."*

Now, Trump may not be entirely to blame here, as the potential use of chloroquine had already been mentioned on Fox News and also tweeted by Spacex founder Elon Musk to his near 32 million followers. Fox News even followed up the story online with an article carrying the headline, *"Drug cleared by Trump,*

FDA for coronavirus testing also found in fish tanks."

Donald Trump has 76 million followers on Twitter, the White House briefings during the COVID-19 pandemic were seen by an average of 8.5 million people each time, and Fox News boasts weekly ratings of over 4 million people. It is no surprise that so many people believed this game-changing misinformation to be true.

Five days after the initial briefing, one woman from Arizona, who remains anonymous, realised that she and her husband had a form of chloroquine at home. She is quoted as saying:

"I saw it sitting on the back shelf and thought, Hey, isn't that the stuff they're talking about on TV?"

The couple reportedly poured some of the chemical into a soda and drank it.

The substance that they found was the fish tank-cleaning chemical, chloroquine phosphate, that is used to treat aquatic parasites. Although it contains the same active ingredient as the drug used for malaria, it is in a different form and can be extremely poisonous to people.

She later explained that their intention was to protect themselves from COVID-19.

"We were afraid of getting sick. Trump kept saying it was basically pretty much a cure," she added.

Thirty minutes after taking the substance, the couple experienced severe reactions that landed them in the emergency department with the husband sadly unable to recover from the damage that the chemical had done.

"Oh my God, don't take anything," she later told the press. *"Don't believe anything that the president says and his people … call your doctor."*

18 INSTANT KARMA

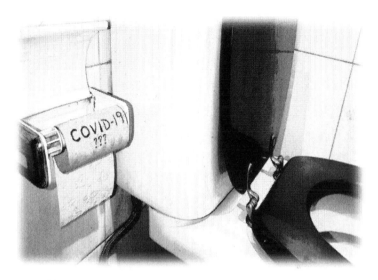

If you believe in the old adage *what goes around, comes around*, then you´ll like the outcome of this story of one complete and utter covidiot from California.

In fact, we come across a couple of covidiots in this story, starting with the TikTok sensation Ava Louise, who recently caused controversy and attracted fierce criticism from all quarters by posting a video titled *"Coronavirus Challenge"*. The disgusting footage showed Louise licking an airplane toilet seat in apparent defiance of all medical sense at a time when COVID-19 was peaking in many countries.

Without a mind of his own, our protagonist, in true copycat style, posted his own version of the Coronavirus Challenge, in which he is recorded licking a public toilet bowl.

Not wanting to mention the 21-year-old "influencer" by name, so as avoid any further unwanted publicity, it became apparent that this brain-dead youth had already shared videos of himself licking ice-cream tubs and spitting into bottles of mouthwash in supermarkets. He even had the audacity to boast about it on a live television show.

Our covidiot has also claimed to have made *"lots of money"* from sponsorship deals and when questioned about his personal life said:

"I don't talk to my family. They´re irrelevant. None of them have followers, if they got followers or got rich I'd probably talk to them again."

However, this brash, arrogant attitude was in stark contrast to the image posted five days after the toilet scene clip. He appeared languishing in a hospital bed after having tested positive for COVID-19, clearly unwell and clearly not a happy little arrogant bunny.

19 TECHNOPHOBIA

With news of the coronavirus breaking around the world in early 2020, conspiracy theories started to spread even faster than the virus itself.

A bio-weapon developed by the Chinese government. A man-made virus accidentally released from a laboratory in Wuhan. A U.S military attack on the Chinese population. The result of peculiar activity between a man and a bat in a cave.

All of these theories have reared their heads to some extent online but the one that stands out above others, and is being lapped up by a worryingly large number of covidiots, is the theory that 5G mobile phone technology is responsible for the spread of COVID-19.

There seems to be two main theories. The first is that 5G suppresses the immune system and makes people more susceptible to catching the virus and suffer more severe reactions.

The second, is that the virus can be somehow transmitted through 5G technology, using radio waves to pick its victims – a theory made more prominent in the media by the fact that a Nobel Prize-winning biologist suggested bacteria could generate radio waves.

These theories spawned Facebook groups supporting these ideas, countless shares and comments on social media, and minor celebrities lending their weight to the argument by posting online. Supporters of the theory claim that they have also seen footage of people *"dropping dead like flies"* in China due to the 5G masts messing with oxygen levels in people´s blood.

All this hype against 5G culminated on the 04th April with the dramatic burning of 5G phone masts in Birmingham and Liverpool in the UK, hopefully not an omen of the civil unrest that is to come!

It´s true that there has been a lot of opposition to mobile phone masts in the past and there are supposed links to certain related health issues, but destroying a means of communication for thousands of people who are required to stay in their own homes and who rely on the internet for work or stay in touch with loved ones, clearly brands these mindless fools as top COVIDIOTS.

20 YOU GOTTA FIGHT FOR YOUR RIGHT TO PARTY

Ah, Spring break! A rite of passage for all young Americans. A time to let your hair down, lose your virginity, puke until you feel like your small intestine is going to pop out, all while trying to avoid ending up in a Mexican jail.

What better way to celebrate the beauty and energy of youth than heading to sun-soaked beaches with your friends, away from the glare of overbearing parents, homework and the pains of being a teenager? What could stop these future leaders of America enjoying their hard-earned vacation?

Well, nothing apparently. Not even a pandemic claiming the lives of tens of thousands of people worldwide and predicted by experts to soon devastate the U.S.A.

As the cases of COVID-19 grew exponentially in March 2020, and social distancing became the new norm, many thousands of spring-breakers ignored the medical advice and set off for places like Florida, Cancun and Cabo San Lucas.

Nothing would stand in their way of having a good time and getting loaded as some party-going covidiots in Miami testified.

"If I get corona, I get corona. At the end of the day, I'm not going to let it stop me from partying. I've been waiting, we've been waiting for Miami spring break for a while. About two months we've had this trip planned, two, three

months, and we're just out here having a good time."

With reference to some closures of public places in resort towns, another added:

"It's really messing up with my spring break. What is there to do here other than go to the bars or the beach? And they're closing all of it. I think they're blowing it way out of proportion. I think it's doing way too much."

Elsewhere, students from the University of Texas in Austin who spent the spring break in Cabo San Lucas, Mexico, didn´t just bring their families back a sombrero or a pair of maracas. Of the 211 young people that went on the trip, more than 50 tested positive for COVID-19, sharing their nasty surprise with unexpecting family members on their return.

I would love to know what their grandparents think of them.

21 WALKING WITH DINOSAURS

On 17th March in the Spanish city of Murcia, inhabitants in the neighbourhood of Vista Alegre were surprised to see a Tyrannosaurus rex waddling down the street carrying a bag of rubbish.

Filmed by one local resident from a balcony, the 6-foot tall theropod was seen, hindered by his tiny forearms, struggling to throw the rubbish bag into a container.

Police arrived on the scene, and despite the man wearing his own form of PPE, was sternly reminded that the city was under a strict COVID-19 lockdown and he didn't have permission to be outside.

The dinosaur-clad curfew-breaker was then seen on the video to uncover his face and reveal his identity to the police before hanging his head in shame, shuffling back to his home with his muscular tail firmly between his legs.

Murcia police later commented on their Twitter account:

*"In a state of alarm, it is permitted for one person to take their dog for a short walk in order for them to do their necessary business. Those who have a **Tyrannosaurus Rex complex are not included in this measure.**"*

22 BITE THE HAND THAT FEEDS

The COVID-19 crisis will give the world something to think about for many years to come and probably provide psychologists with enough samples of different human behaviour to digest for generations.

People have reacted to the virus and its consequences in a huge variety of ways. We've seen generosity, grief, despair, hope, courage, humour, disdain, blame, love, charity, loneliness, laziness, madness and joy, among many other feelings to varying degrees.

We´ve seen people sharing their talents by serenading others from their balconies. We´ve read stories of long-lost relatives finally making contact after many years. We´ve witnessed acts of selflessness that have inspired vast numbers of people to be better. We´ve even finally said hello to the neighbour living in the flat next door to us for the last six years.

But one thing that really stands out among all these human reactions is the anger that we have seen around the world. Of course, not everyone is completely well-balanced and some people´s reactions to something like being confined at home, while not being excused, may be explained in some way.

Nevertheless, the anger we have seen by numerous covidiots around the world towards healthcare workers has shocked most of us.

In the U.K, where a number of National Health Service workers died as a result of the virus, nurses were advised not to travel outside of work wearing their uniforms after some were spat at and called *"disease spreaders"*. There were also reports of them being attacked for their I.D badges as desperate people look to get a free hot or cold drink at McDonalds or 50% off PERi-PERi chicken at Nando's, posing as NHS staff.

The anti-healthcare worker sentiment was also evident in Colombia, the United States, Spain, Italy and particularly in India, where some workers were kicked and spat at, chased away from their homes and even had stones thrown at them.

In a country where reincarnation is a central religious belief, we can only hope that these covidiots appear in another life in the form that they deserve.

23   YES, PRIME MINISTER

When COVID-19 started to spread at an alarming rate outside China at the beginning of March 2020, many countries shut up shop, the military were deployed and travel in and out of nations was strictly denied to all but a few citizens returning home.

However, the British government saw things a bit differently. Not liking to be told what to do by other nations, the cabinet followed the advice of its own top scientists by allowing the virus to spread naturally among the population, in an approach that was known as *"Herd immunity"*. The idea was that by flattening the curve of infections with controlled exposure to the disease, Britain would ease the long-term consequences of the pandemic.

British Prime Minister, Boris Johnson, advocate of such great, game-changing ideas in the past as Brexit, told the British public that it was basically business as usual and even boasted, *"I shook hands with everybody"*, after visiting patients, some of whom were suffering from coronavirus, on a hospital visit.

On top of this, Boris had also missed five consecutive emergency meetings in late January and February, held to discuss a plan of action for the COVID-19 crisis, and was accused by the opposition Labour Party of being *"missing in action"*.

Eventually, in mid-March, based on solid medical analysis this time, the British government ordered a U-turn on their herd immunity theory, ordering non-essential businesses to shut and people to stay at home.

On 27th March, Mr Johnson went into self-isolation, showing symptoms of COVID-19, and on 05th April was admitted to hospital. At the time of writing, he is still in intensive care in St Thomas´ Hospital, London. We sincerely wish him the very best for a full and speedy recovery.

By this stage of the crisis, the Prime Minister´s pregnant fiancée was now showing symptoms of the coronavirus and Britain had seen nearly five thousand deaths and forty-eight thousand infections, with rates continuing to rise rapidly.

Apparently, the virus had little respect for a go-it-alone attitude and the great British resolve, which have been pillars of society since Winston Churchill urged his fellow countrymen to fight their enemies on the beaches, the fields, and the streets of this *"green and pleasant land."*

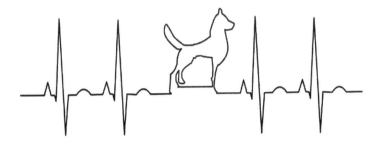

The COVID-19 crisis has made people think long and hard about many things. One of which is the relationship we have with our canine companions. There have been many stories circulating in the media and going viral related to dogs, some more covidiotic than others.

Although difficult to verify 100%, there were reports from many places that applications for dog adoptions rose significantly during the first few months of 2020.

Many countries employed strict lockdown measures with few people being allowed out of their homes, with the exception of essential service workers and those taking dogs for walks. Animal shelters were therefore apparently inundated with people looking for an excuse to get outside and stretch their legs without the risk of facing a fine.

One man in Palencia, Spain, that wanted such dog-walking privileges, was spotted by residents apparently dragging a small puppy along the pavement quite brusquely. A local resident, suspicious of the man´s activities and fearing the animal was suffering some form of mistreatment, notified the police. Upon arrival, it was clear to the authorities that this covidiot was trying his best to fool them and break curfew. He was given a stern caution, escorted back to his home and told to give the fluffy toy back to his daughter.

On the other hand, one man in Cyprus, not wanting to leave the safety of his home to take his dog out, made use of a drone to give his pet its exercise. The images were seen close to 4 million times online, with many people wondering just how the drone would manage with a poo bag.

Another stay-at-home quarantiner in Mexico, Antonio Muñoz, had such a craving for crisps that he sent his little chihuahua, Chokis, to the local shop to get him a packet of Cheetos. Images showed the apparently frightened little thing with a $20 bill and a note stuffed into its collar, which read:

"Hello sir of the store, can you sell my dog some orange – not red – Cheetos. In his collar, he brings $20. If you don't take good care of my dog, he will bite. From, the neighbour across the street."

It worked a treat and Chokis was sent on many further runs to the shops.

As dogs which normally jumped for joy at the sight of their lead cowered behind the sofa, not wanting to be taken out for yet another walk by a different family member looking for an excuse to escape the curfew, the COVID-19 crisis, on the whole, highlighted what a special relationship we really have with our four-legged friends.

As for me, I sent my cat out for a packet of Jaffa Cakes last Tuesday but haven´t seen him since.

25 SHAME ON YOU

Corona-shaming started to appear as people were forced to change their habits or stay in their homes in many parts of the world as the virus took hold.

Angry reactions to people not applauding health service workers from their balconies, people being abused and then trolled online if they were accompanied to the supermarket by another person, and even projectiles being thrown down on suspected curfew breakers in some neighbourhoods were all reported by the media.

In one country, where only a single person from any household could go outside at any one time, shouts of *"Have you no shame?"* and *"get the coronavirus and die!"* were directed at people, including frightened parents who in fact had permission to take their autistic children out for a walk as part of their therapy.

Governments didn´t do a lot to discourage this atmosphere of shame and blame, with the New Zealand authorities asking their citizens to "dob in" self-isolation breakers and quarantine-flouting tourists, leading to an ugly atmosphere of *them and us* in the country.

Asking citizens to be the eyes and ears of the government sets a dangerous precedent and effectively gives anyone, mentally stable or not, "permission" to take the law into their own hands and act as vigilantes. Something we unfortunately experienced first-hand there.

In India, things were taken a step further though, with some police publicly shaming those they found not respecting the initial 21-day curfew, which came into effect on the 25th March, 2020.

The humiliation ranged from making offenders do squats, sit-ups, push-ups and even crawl along the street. One had *"I have violated lockdown restrictions, keep away from me"* written on his forehead by a friendly permanent marker-wielding policeman. Others were made to wear masks in the shape of the virus in microscopic form and some had signs hung around their necks that read:

"I am a friend of coronavirus.", "Some people do not care about society's safety.", "I do not believe in the law of the country" and *"I do not care about my family or society."*

However, it could be a lot worse for law-breaking citizens. Philippine President Rodrigo Duterte, broadcast to the nation this message:

"I will not hesitate. My orders are to the police and military, as well as village officials, if there is any trouble, or occasions where there's violence and your lives are in danger, SHOOT THEM DEAD. Is that understood? Dead. Instead of causing trouble, I will bury you."

Message received loud and clear Mr Duterte.

26　WE SHALL NOT BE MOVED

COVID-19 caught tens of thousands of people working, studying or holidaying, often far away from their country of origin. Many were forced to change their travel plans and return home early, while others found themselves stranded and had to get back as best they could.

The vast majority of people abroad followed the instructions of the local authorities without complaint, even if it meant staying in their accommodation as lockdowns became commonplace, until they were able to fly back home.

Some British tourists in the Spanish resort town of Benidorm, famous for its beautiful beaches, package holidays, Irish pubs and evening entertainment such as the infamous "Sticky Vicky", didn´t take kindly to being told what to, however.

When Spanish police politely asked the holidaymakers to *"please go back to the safety of your apartment"*, their request seemed to fall on deaf ears.

"It's just a flu that you need to get over - have a beer, happy days, ciao guys." One half-naked, drunk British man responded as other tourists pushed shopping trolleys full of alcohol down the street.

Another piped up and said, *"We´re flying home soon"*. As if it gave him the right to carry on drinking as much as possible in public.

The most shameful images, though, must be of the 50 or so, mostly drunk, some topless, tourists that refused to go back to their accommodation and chanted at the police, who were trying to keep order, *"We´ve all got the virus, we´ve all got the virus, la la la la…la la la la."*

Compatriots of the Benidorm covidiots were also pulled out of swimming pools in other parts of the country in defiance of the new laws, including one woman in Tenerife in the Canary Islands, filmed doing roly-polies in the pool in protest of the public areas being closed at her hotel. Police officers were forced to jump in and drag her out against her will as she splashed around like a demented manatee.

What kind of irresponsible person would do this sort of thing, showing blatant disregard for the authorities and the safety of others?

Well, it turns out that the woman in question, Joanne Rust, was a political candidate for the Labour Party in the U.K and ran for office at the last general election.

27 FOLLOW THE LEADER

We´ve already seen how some world leaders successfully self-promoted themselves as proper covidiots, so let´s take a look at what a few others got up to as COVID-19 progressed.

Everyone´s favourite shiny shell-suit wearing South American politician (believe it or not, there are actually a few out there), Nicolás Maduro, hit the headlines again on the 22nd March 2020, when he felt he had to share the message of controversial Venezuelan scientist, Sirio Quintero.

President of Venezuela, Maduro tweeted comments attributed to Quintero, referring to the virus as a weapon of *"bio-terrorism"*. Maduro quotes his trusted scientist on his Twitter account, adding that the coronavirus is:

"An expression of the highest scientific and technological capacity reached by the nuclei of the imperial powers in their handbook of bioterrorism."

He explains his theory in more detail by saying:

"The coronavirus is designed in laboratories in order to specifically attack the organs in the human body of the Chinese and ethnic Latin American races."

Maduros´s tweet continues with the wise words of Mr Quintero, *"drink five glasses a day during twelve weeks, a potion of lemongrass, ripe lemon juice and honey."*

Sounds like pretty good advice to me. I´ll send Chokis over to the store with a shopping list.

Elsewhere in Latin America, the advice just keeps coming. *"We're going to keep living life as usual,"* Mexican president Andrés Manuel López Obrador insisted publicly.

"I'll tell you when not to go out any longer." In the meantime, he recommended that, "If you're able and have the means to do so, continue taking your family out to eat … because that strengthens the economy." He also endorsed *"hugging and kissing"* your family in a time of crisis.

Obrador´s advice to his people is in sharp contrast to countries that successfully managed to get COVID-19 under control at an early stage. South Korean authorities imposed strict measures from the outset and even recommended that individual family members wear facemasks at home and try to be in separate rooms from the rest of their family, even if they were asymptomatic.

History will tell what the best approach was.

And finally, what would any revered monarch do to show solidarity with their loyal subjects? Don a face mask and visit hospitals to support medical staff and bring hope to the sick, like King Filipe VI of Spain? Broadcast a special address to the nation for only the fourth time in history offering words of courage and solidarity, as Queen Elizabeth II did on 05th April 2020?

Or take over an entire luxury hotel in the alpine resort town of Garmisch-Partenkirchen, Germany with your servants and 20 concubines? Well, that´s exactly what Thailand's King Maha Vajiralongkorn, also known as Roger Moore, sorry, Rama X, did.

Self-isolation can be hard for some people, indeed. Not quite as hard as the backlash that Rama X will face when he gets back to Thailand, where the movement *"Why do we need a king?"* is gathering pace with now close to 2 million supporters.

How would you feel if your actions forced one of the world´s biggest sports competitions into premature closure, prompting the rest of the sporting world to follow suit shortly afterwards?

Pretty damn sorry I would imagine. And thankfully that is how Utah Jazz´s Rudy Gobert felt after his actions left him with some explaining to do.

On March 09th 2020, the French basketball star was filmed at the end of a press conference, jokingly touching the microphones and recording equipment in front of him in apparent mockery of how the deadly virus could be transmitted.

Two days later, he tested positive for COVID-19, the first NBA player to do so. The NBA basketball competition was subsequently stopped and he faced the wrath of the public and fellow basketball players alike, accusing him of insensitivity at a time when thousands were dying.

A repentant Gobert later published the following statement:

"The first and most important thing is I would like to publicly apologize to the people that I may have endangered. At the time, I had no idea I was even infected. I was careless and make no excuse. I hope my story serves as a

warning and causes everyone to take this seriously. I will do whatever I can to support using my experience as way to educate others and prevent the spread of this virus. I am under great care and will fully recover."

"Thank you again for all your support. I encourage everyone to take all of the steps to stay safe and healthy. Love."

In an attempt to clean his tarnished image, Gobert pledged $500,000 to coronavirus-related relief efforts, $200,000 to part-time Jazz arena employees impacted by the loss of games at the venue, $100,000 to help families affected by the COVID-19 pandemic in both Utah and Oklahoma City, and €100,000 back in his native France.

29 MINISTER OF (NO) DEFENSE

We have to apologize, but stories about politicians keep popping up here as it appears that they just can´t help themselves when it comes to demonstrating just what a bunch of covidiots many of them seem to be.

The latest in our hall of shame is the New Zealand health minister David Clark.

New Zealand went into a strict lockdown on the 25th March 2020, and apart from a few surfers and a group of bridge-jumpers, people pretty much abided by the rules during the initial four-week period as the country remained relatively unscathed in comparison to much of the rest of the world.

The kiwi government made great pains to emphasise the importance of staying at home and only going out for essentials and exercise in your "family bubble", and in your immediate local area.

OK, the rules should apply to everyone, including young surfers that may feel they are doing no harm catching a few waves. However, some people in particular should be setting a great example to the rest of the population.

Mr Clark had already broken the lockdown rules (which included not participating in activities that may cause injury and therefore place extra burden on hospitals) he himself was partly responsible for implementing, when on the 02nd April he drove 2km to go mountain biking. Now, he might have got away with it had his van not been parked all alone in a car park and if it didn´t have a one and a half metre campaign photograph of his grinning face emblazoned on the side.

His wrists firmly slapped by Prime Minister Jacinda Ardern, what does Mr Clark do four days later? He drives his whole family 20km to the suitably named Doctor´s Point beach in ANOTHER clear breach of the rules.

An angry Ardern immediately dealt with the covidiot, stripping him of his Associate Finance ministry role and demoted him to the bottom of the Cabinet rankings.

In a statement to the press, Ardern said:

"Under normal conditions, I would sack the minister of health. What he did was wrong, and there are no excuses."

"But right now, my priority is our collective fight against COVID-19. We cannot afford

massive disruption in the health sector or to our response. For that reason, and that reason alone, Dr Clark will maintain his role."

"But he does need to pay a price. He broke the rules."

Clark, who is expected to lose his role as Health Minister when the COVID-19 crisis comes to an end, responded that he felt:

"Like a complete dick to be honest".

30 DIRTY CASH

Ever since it was discovered that strains of COVID-19 could survive on various surfaces for not just hours, but in some cases a number of days, the general public and governments alike, embarked upon an unprecedented cleaning frenzy.

We all saw the images of armies of workers in protective clothing dousing public places with disinfectant or marching through cinema aisles in a cloud of bleach-ridden vapour, inspiring more people than ever to stay at home and watch Netflix from the safety of their own sofa.

After learning that the virus could remain present on paper for up to five days, some governments then turned their attention to disinfecting paper currency. Chinese, South Korean and Hungarian governments all took large amounts of bank notes out of circulation, placed them under quarantine for up to two weeks, and then processed them to remove any trace of the virus.

In Georgia, where such a scheme had not been implemented, one market in the Black Sea port town of Poti made shoppers hand over their bank notes to be ironed at the entrance, in order for the virus to be killed by high temperatures, while coins were washed with a special sterilizing solution.

Meanwhile, in Russia, one woman, who learnt about the infectious potential of cash, decided to try to use the heat sterilization method herself...with her microwave. Placing various wads of roubles in the domestic appliance, she had obviously overseen the fact that most paper money these days has a metal security thread running through it. She ended up with her very own mini fourth of July in her kitchenette and piles of smoking, worthless money.

In total, she destroyed 65,000 roubles (around 850 US dollars). About what it cost to buy two packets of loo roll and a bottle of hand sanitiser at that time.

31   FREE HUGS

The relationship between the Spanish government and the few Catalan politicians that support independence in the north-eastern autonomous region of Cataluña has grown increasingly strained over recent years.

Popularist pro-Catalan parties, despite never gaining a majority of support in Cataluña itself, have continued to try to divide Spain and its citizens and foster an atmosphere of resentment towards the Spanish central government.

At a time when solidarity was sorely needed, instead of healing the wounds created by the drive for independence and working together against a common enemy, one local Catalan politician encouraged the exact opposite.

Using Twitter to share his feelings, Joan Coma of the CUP party, directed his anger towards the army, which was on its way to disinfect public areas in the region of Cataluña, including the Airport in Barcelona and various retirement homes. He wrote:

"If we see the army, we´ll hug them hard, coughing in their faces. Maybe that way they´ll leave here and not come back", he encouraged anyone stupid enough to follow him online.

Coma had previously come out with other pearls of wisdom when referring to Catalan independence, such as:

"If you want to make an omelette you need to break some eggs."

And, *"We understand disobedience as a tool to force the change to self-governance that will also improve the democracy in the whole country."*

COVID-19 wreaked havoc on the economy worldwide and particularly in Spain in 2020. Cataluña, and especially Barcelona, were extremely badly hit with infections and have relied heavily on the financial aid provided by the central government, which was divided between the autonomous regions in the country.

How would an independent Cataluña cope with an economic depression on a grand scale? Especially if they were not part of the European Union, as would be the case if secession were achieved without a proper legal process involving Spain.

The Catalan people are an educated, inventive and hard-working bunch with a great deal to offer the world.

However, it´s headline-grabbing covidiots like Joan Coma and a handful of other politicians intent of leaving their own legacy, which threaten to do more long-term damage to this beautiful part of Spain than COVID-19 ever could.

32 LOVE IN A TIME OF CORONAVIRUS

Our next Covidiot let something else rather than his head make decisions for him as an infidelity led to an entire town being placed under quarantine in Argentina.

In mid-March 2020, all 2,500 residents of the northern Argentinian town Selva found themselves housebound, while shops, restaurants and other businesses were forced to close.

The man in question, a 27-year-old Selva resident, had got back in touch with an old flame from years before and so she invited him to meet her in the city of Cordoba, 400km to the south.

Our Casanova shot down to meet her and despite the fact that she had been honest and told him she had just returned from Spain with symptoms of COVID-19, they got it on. Obviously, the hacking dry cough was not a turn-off.

Upon returning to his hometown, his friends threw a party. It is unclear if it was held in honour of his exploits down south, but whatever the reason was, he started to boast about his encounter with his former lover.

He also let it slip that she was suffering from Coronavirus symptoms, (why on earth would you do that?) of which his friends were shocked to hear about and quickly dobbed him in to the authorities.

Just a couple of days later, Selva Governor Gerardo Zamora, had isolated the town from the rest of the country, neither allowing anyone to enter, nor to leave. The woman was located and placed in isolation in Cordoba, along with her husband.

In hindsight, the Selva resident may have done his town a favour, keeping the population safely inside away from the possibility of infection from other sources, but tell that to the local businesses that lost their livelihoods prematurely. Or the husband of the lady from Cordoba.

Lockdowns took various forms in different countries around the world at the beginning of 2020. Some places restricted their citizens to almost complete isolation, while others allowed people to go outside and exercise in "their own bubble", which was largely very open to interpretation.

What we did witness in some countries that still allowed a certain degree of freedom of movement at the start of the crisis, were urbanites heading to the countryside to escape densely populated areas with a supposedly high risk of contagion, and people travelling to their holiday homes on the coast.

In the U.K, beauty spots, beaches and small villages saw an influx of tourists and motorhomes, the extent of which was never seen before. Some areas were visited by up to 80% more people than normal.

The U.S.A also saw many national parks inundated with RVs and people looking to get fresh air, instead of breathing in the germs that were rife in their own apartments in the towns and cities.

Now, fleeing to areas with many other visitors from all over the country, little medical facilities, few shops, and locals that are more likely to do to you with a pitchfork what COVID-19 never could, doesn´t really seem like a bright idea.

Aside from the lack of resources in the countryside, the resentment towards, out-of-towners or foreigners stuck abroad struggling to get home, started to be witnessed. If this were in another era, the locals would be pulling their wagons into a circle, armed to the teeth, waiting for their Alamo moment.

We saw signs, telling people to "bugger off" and roads blocked with concrete slabs and even huge piles of manure, as farming communities looked to keep their villages virus-free. More worrying maybe is at the higher end of the scale, with many governments telling foreigners to go home and that they would only care for their own citizens should COVID-19 get out of control. All of which has fostered a feeling of nationalism, racism and prejudice around the globe.

New Zealand, for example, has been held up in the international press as an example of one of the countries to have best handled the COVID-19 crisis. However, at the beginning of the restrictions imposed, New Zealanders, unlike other nationalities, didn't have to do a mandatory quarantine, irrespective of which country they had returned from, as if their nationality could protect them from infection or transmission.

Although there is some evidence which suggests that people from black and minority ethnic backgrounds are dying in disproportionate numbers, your nationality, on the other hand, cannot protect you from infection or transmission, nor should it allow you to be exempt from certain measures.

So, what does the future hold for society in post COVID-19 times?

We've heard many people claiming that their self-isolation or lockdown period will make them better people. We sincerely hope so. We hope that people come out the other end of this crisis showing the same solidarity they have done in these times with acts such as putting rainbows painted by their children in windows or with the daily or weekly applauding in support of health-service workers.

If these demonstrations of solidarity can continue to spread into meaningful actions in the future and are not just used to boost an Instagram or Facebook profile or show neighbours how conscientious we are while under lockdown, then the world will surely be a better place for all of us.

34   THE SHOW MUST GO ON

Our final story from Spain brings us to the small Andalucian town of Villamartin in the province of Cadiz, on Palm Sunday, 2020.

Even though gatherings in public were banned, 05th April saw 10,300 people fined and 100 individuals detained by the police. Among whom, were three people responsible for the recreation of the *procesión de la Borriquita,* an important Easter parade held nationwide.

The Spanish take Easter seriously, unlike these three, whose parody of the popular procession went viral.

Complete with shawl, palm leaf, flowers, rosary and riding what appeared to be a stuffed toy donkey, the satire carried out by the couple, accompanied by a cameraperson, was near perfect.

One of the most famous scenes depicted in Easter parades, our covidiots re-enacted *The triumphal entry of Jesus to Jerusalem*, to the background of typical trumpet music that is commonplace at this time of year.

The only problem was, that killjoy police didn´t take too kindly to these illegal processionists and broke up the impromptu parade, much to the disappointment of neighbours who had come to doors, windows and balconies to enjoy the holy entertainment.

35 TRUMP

Where do we begin? What can this man do that doesn´t surprise people these days? Without risking a costly libel lawsuit, it´s probably best that we leave you with some of Mr Trump´s very own chronologically listed quotes about COVID-19 and you judge for yourself how he handled things.

"We have it totally under control. It's one person coming in from China, and we have it under control. It's going to be just fine."

22nd January

"We think we have it very well under control. We have very little problem in this country at this moment — five — and those people are all recuperating successfully. But we're working very closely with China and other countries, and we think it's going to have a very good ending for us … that I can assure you."

30th January

"Looks like by April, you know, in theory, when it gets a little warmer, it miraculously goes away."

10th February

"The Coronavirus is very much under control in the USA. … Stock Market starting to look very good to me!"

24th February

"And again, when you have 15 people, and the 15 within a couple of days is going to be down to close to zero, that's a pretty good job we've done."

26th February

"It's going to disappear. One day, it's like a miracle, it will disappear."

28th February

"Some people will have this at a very light level and won't even go to a doctor or hospital, and they'll get better. There are many people like that."

04th March

"No, I'm not concerned at all. No, we've done a great job with it."

07th March

"We're prepared, and we're doing a great job with it. In addition, it will go away. Just stay calm. It will go away."

10th March

WHO Declares COVID-19 pandemic.

11TH March

"We're using the full power of the federal government to defeat the virus, and that's what we've been doing."

14TH March

"This is a very contagious virus. It's incredible. But it's something that we have tremendous control over."

15th March

"I felt it was a pandemic long before it was called a pandemic."

17th March

"I always treated the Chinese Virus very seriously, and have done a very good job from the beginning, including my very early decision to close the 'borders' from China - against the wishes of almost all."

18th March

"You look at automobile accidents, which are far greater than any numbers we're talking about. That doesn't mean we're going to tell everybody no more driving of cars. So we have to do things to get our country open."

23rd March

"America will again, and soon, be open for business — very soon — a lot sooner than three

or four months that somebody was suggesting. ... We cannot let the cure be worse than the problem itself."

23rd March

"I'd love to have the country opened up and just raring to go by Easter."

24th March

"WE WILL WIN THIS WAR. When we achieve this victory, we will emerge stronger and more united than ever before!"

28th March

"Nothing would be worse than declaring victory before the victory is won."

29th March

117

This collection of stories about covidiots was cobbled together at the beginning of April 2020. God only knows what else Donald Trump would have said by the time the crisis is finally under control or this book finds itself into your hands.

One thing for sure is that from a journalistic point of view, Mr Trump never fails to satisfy those looking for column inches.

However, his ineptitude and failure to strike while the iron was hot when clear medical advice was present, may just leave its indelible mark on American society for many years to come.

36 DON'T TRY THIS AT HOME

And so, we come to our final round-up of some of the home remedies and myths that have been tried to keep COVID-19 at bay.

With testing kits being a prized commodity for most governments, along with the fact that many have turned up either unreliable or packed in boxes with the decomposing corpses of dead animals rendering them unusable, many people ended up trying a self-diagnosis technique that was being touted online.

Apparently, if you could hold your breath for more than 10 seconds without the need to cough or feel discomfort, you were disease free. This technique was quickly dismissed by the WHO as reports of side effects such as light-headedness and blackouts were reported.

Other people turned to the excessive consumption of alcohol in order to try to sterilize their insides. If it works for cleaning the hands, why can´t it make you a super-immune human if you sweat the stuff? Supermarket sales of booze went up by about 80% in some places, although it is not clear if this was a result of the rumour or being under lockdown with close relatives.

In Turkey meanwhile, rubbing alcohol was promoted as a means of killing the virus, and while it can be used topically to kill bugs, something may have been lost in translation, leading to the unfortunate death of 20 people who drank the substance.

Some people avoided using contact lenses, as it was proved that the disease could be transmitted by infected droplets entering the eyes. While this advice was not bad at all as we know that we should avoid touching anywhere around our face, it may have led to a reported rise in household accidents with the combination of visually-impaired people staying at home and the increase in the use of kitchen appliances.

Drinking lots of warm water, gargling with a saline solution, and inhaling steam were also mentioned quite a lot on the internet, and being treatments for things like sinusitis and the common cold, they won't do you any harm if you suffer from these common ailments.

However, steam is actually believed to propagate the Coronavirus infection throughout the lungs, causing more harm than good.

In short, these home treatments will not prevent or treat COVID-19. (Neither will sheep´s head soup nor ringing bells, by the way)

Another theory that was lent weight by studies in the scientific community was that in hotter or more humid countries the Coronavirus didn´t spread so rapidly or have such severe symptoms.

This caused a wave of people taking piping hot baths, wearing multiple layers of thermal clothing and huge overcoats, and even attempting to increase their core temperature with hairdryers at home or by using hand dryers in public toilets – something quite tricky to do with a Dyson Airblade I can tell you.

As we write this book, most of the world is still in lockdown for the first time in its history, and maybe today, as you read this, due to COVID-19, COVID-20 or COVID-32, you still are.

So, if you find yourself cocooned in bubble wrap, breathing through a snorkel with a coffee filter stuffed in the end, while intravenously injecting a combination of ginger, turmeric and kombucha, take a good look at yourself and consider if you really are just one more covidiot.

APPENDIX

Sources of photographs and images:

1 - Image by Clker-Free-Vector- Images from Pixabay.

2 - Image by OpenClipart-Vectors from Pixabay.

3 - Image by Beverly Buckley from Pixabay.

4 - Image by Iberia Airlines flight crew, released by Fiscalía, Ecuador. 19/03/2020

5 - Image by OpenClipart-Vectors from Pixabay.

6 - Image by stopic from Pixabay

7 - Image by Alexas Fotos from Pixabay.

8 - Image by S B from Pixabay

9 - Image by Jahir Martinez on Unsplash

10 - Image by OpenClipart-Vectors from Pixabay

11 - Image by John Cameron on Unsplash.

12 - Image by Richard Tao on Unsplash

13 - Image by Oskar Kadaksoo on Unsplash.

14 - Image by Clker-Free-Vector-Images from Pixabay.

15 - Image by Magnascan from Pixabay.

16 - Image by OpenClipart-Vectors from Pixabay.

17 - Image by Gerd Altmann from Pixabay

18 - Author's own image.

19 - Image by Jack Sloop on Unsplash.

20 - Image by Laura Fuhrman on Unsplash.

21 - Photo by José Luis Photographer from Pexels,

22 - Image by OpenClipart-Vectors from Pixabay.

23- Image by Clker-Free-Vector Images from Pixabay.

24 - Image by Gordon Johnson from Pixabay.

25 - Image by Gerd Altmann from Pixabay.

26 - Image by Pixaline from Pixabay.

27 - Image by Steve Watts from Pixabay.

28 - Image by OpenClipart-Vectors from Pixabay.

29 - Image by Alice Hartrick on Unsplash.

30 - Author´s own image.

31 - Image by Alexas Fotos from Pixabay.

32 - Image by (微博/微信) 愚木混株 Instagram cdd20 from Pixabay

33 - Image by Thanks for your Like • donations welcome from Pixabay.

34 - Image by Vidar Nordli-Mathisen on Unsplash.

35 - Image by BarBus from Pixabay.

36 - Image by Ferdinand Studio from Pexels.

Front cover - Edited image by Cottombro from Pexels
Back cover - Image by Syaibatul Hamdi from Pixabay.